THE BEGINNINGS OF THE LABOR UNIONS

History Book for Kids 9-12
Children's History

What are labor unions, and how did they start? Let's put on our hard hats and our overalls and go find out!

EARLY LABOR GROUPS

Medieval craftsmen were the only workers in Europe with organizations, which were often called guilds, and they were both a social society and a training system for people who worked in a particular skilled trade. A town might have a guild for weavers, one for leather-makers, and so on. Each guild might have its own meeting-place to hold feasts and other events. The guild would guard trade secrets, such as special formulas, and pushed governments to protect their products from competition with goods made in other countries.

When a family wanted to help a child get a career, they could apprentice the child to a member of one of the guilds. The child would work first a menial jobs, and then help more and more with the important work, doing hands-on learning.

The guilds were a powerful feature of medieval Europe, and could get better working conditions and pay for their members. But they were more like a professional association than a union—the modern equivalent might be an association of doctors or lawyers. The great majority of people in medieval Europe did manual labor on farms or in towns. They were paid very little and had no protections if they fell ill or if their employer abused them.

THE PEASANTS' REVOLT

Periodically, workers rose up to try to win better conditions for themselves. In 1381 most of England experienced the Peasants' Revolt, also known as Wat Tyler's Rebellion after one of its leaders. A court official tried to collect some unpaid taxes in a high-handed way. Workers, and even leaders of town governments, joined in an armed rebellion. The goals of the rebellion were lower taxes and an end to serfdom, the system of unpaid labor under which most English farm laborers worked. The revolt was put down with violence, and several thousand people died in the fighting.

LABOR AND THE INDUSTRIAL REVOLUTION

However, not much changed in the relationship between employers and laborers until the industrial revolution in the eighteenth century in Europe and the nineteenth century in North America.

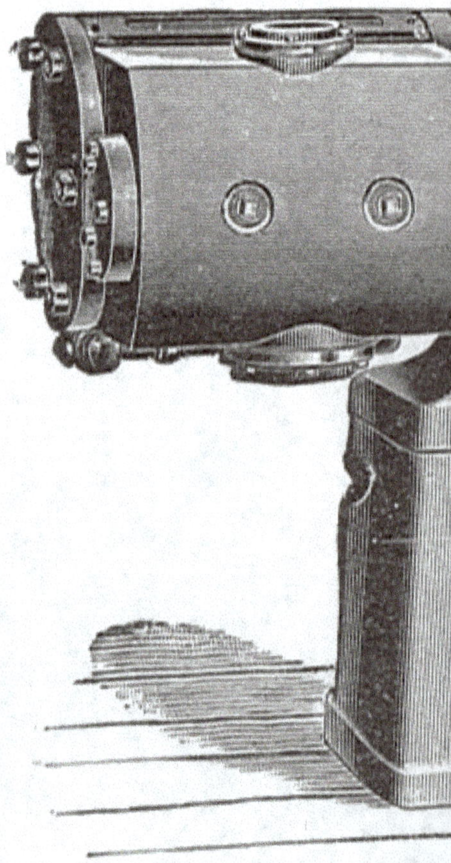

Invention of energy sources like the steam engine and water-powered turbines, along with new tools like automated weaving looms, led to factories springing up in cities and towns.

People who had done piece-work in their homes could now move to a town and get a job in a factory. Although the pay was low and the conditions were harsh, people's lives were often better and with more options than they had been when they were living in rural isolation, forced to work under one landowner.

As factory workers grew in number, they became essential to the manufacturing process. If the workers did not work, the machines could not run and the product would not be made. This gave the workers some ability to press for better working conditions, higher pay, and better treatment. The efforts were not always successful, as factory owners saw any gain by the workers as costly.

In the United States, the early colonies had trades associations that were much like medieval guilds. They met for social purposes and for training, and organized their apprenticeship system.

The first recorded strike in North America was in 1768. The tailors of New York stopped work to protest a reduction in their pay rate.

CORDWAINER

In 1794 in Philadelphia, shoemakers formed the Federal Society of Journeymen Cordwainers, the first union for American workers, as opposed to a guild or society for higher-trained specialists like lawyers.

From then, many local craft unions appeared in cities. Its members would publish standard prices for typical jobs they would do (so much to put a new sole on a boot, so much more to repair the leather where it is ripped, and so on). They defended their members and their products against the sale of cheaper goods made by less-skilled workers, and pressed for a shorter work day. The work day at the start of 1800 was about ten hours each weekday, plus several hours on Saturday.

SAAPAS

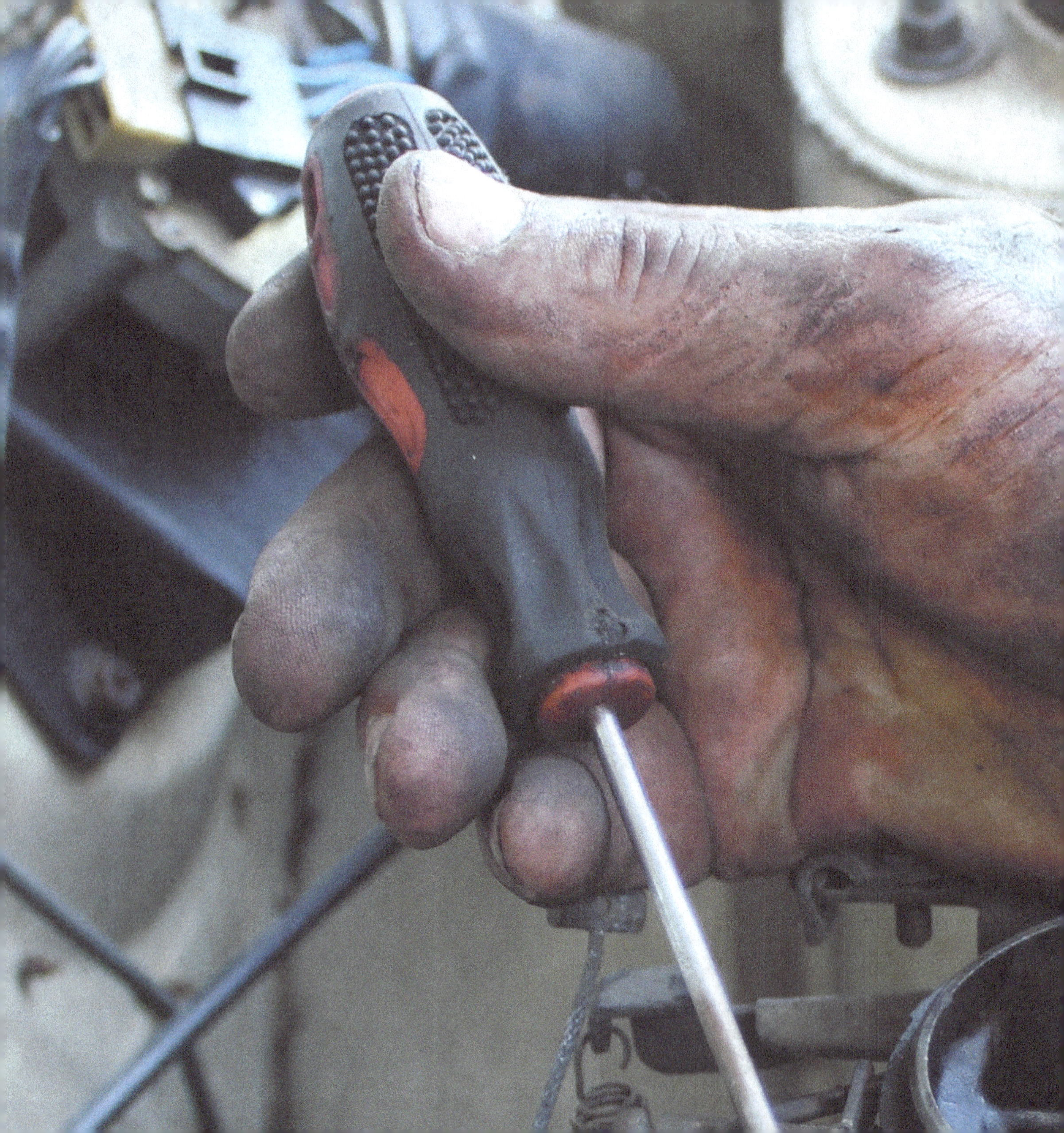

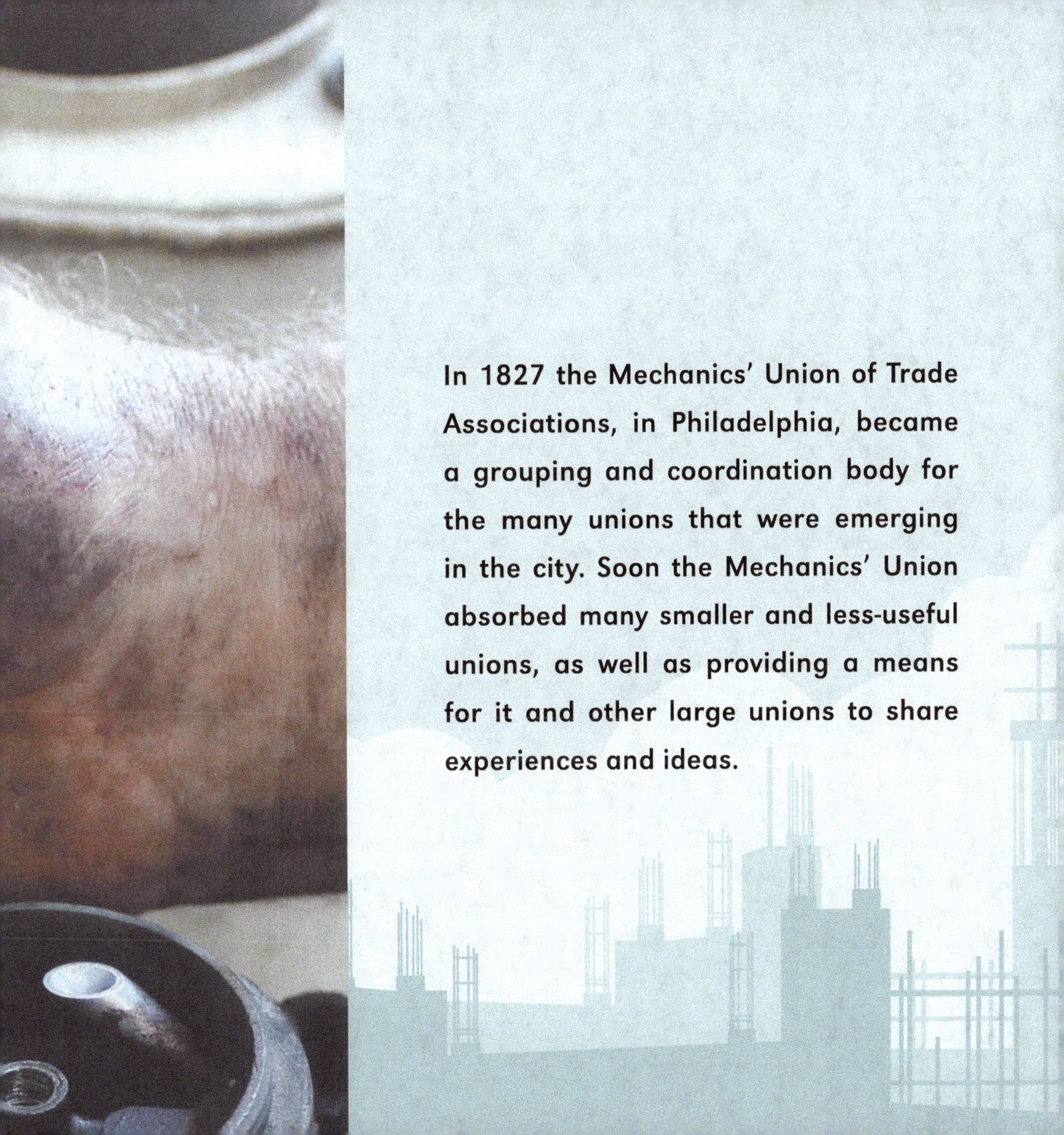

In 1827 the Mechanics' Union of Trade Associations, in Philadelphia, became a grouping and coordination body for the many unions that were emerging in the city. Soon the Mechanics' Union absorbed many smaller and less-useful unions, as well as providing a means for it and other large unions to share experiences and ideas.

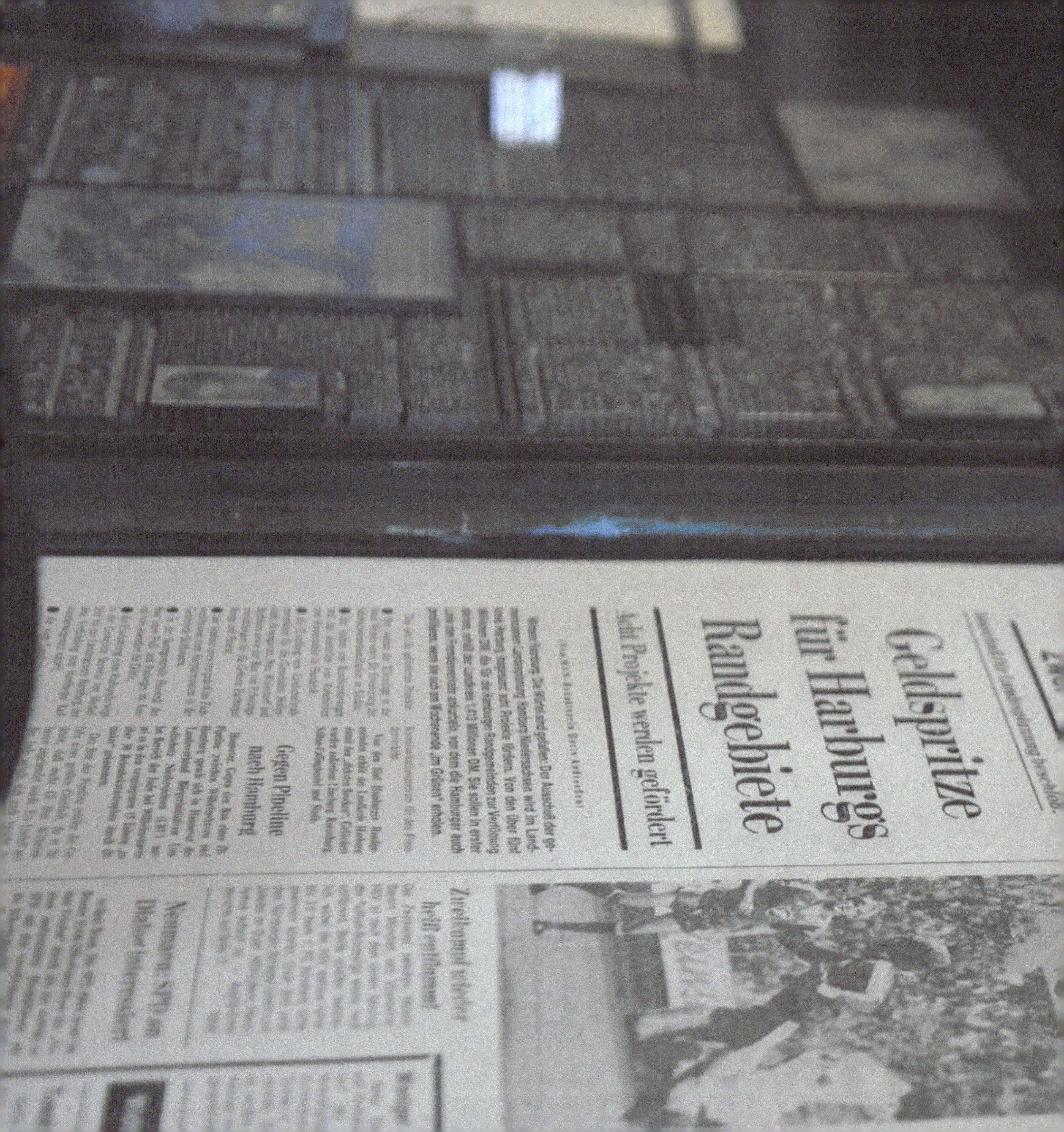

Geldspritze für Harburgs Randgebiete

Acht Projekte werden gefördert

(Von HAN-Redakteurin Doris Andresen)

Raum Hamburg. Die Würfel sind gefallen: Der Ausschuß der gemeinsamen Landesplanung Hamburg/Niedersachsen wird im Landkreis Harburg insgesamt acht Projekte fördern. Von den über fünf Millionen DM, die für die Hamburger Randgemeinden zur Verfügung stehen, erhält der Landkreis 1,412 Millionen DM. Sie sollen in erster Linie den Fremdenverkehr ankurbeln; von dem die Hamburger auch profitieren, wenn sie sich am Wochenende „im Grünen" erholen.

Gegen Pipeline nach Hamburg

Hannover. Gegen den Bau einer Öl-Pipeline zwischen Wilhelmshaven und Hamburg spricht sich in Hannover die Landtreffend-Fraktion der niedersächsischen Niedersachsen (LRT) an. Im Bereich der Isch bei Wilhelmshaven werde auch die „Edeka-Senker" Geländestreifen Lüneburg, Buxtehude, Lüneburg und Stade.

Zweikampf wieder heiß entflammt

Neumann: SPD an Dialog interessiert

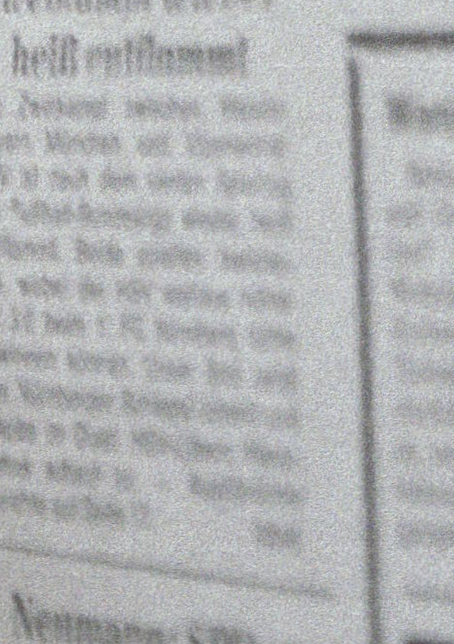

The next step was in 1852. The International Typographical Union was created by merging a large number of related unions in not just one city, but all across the United States and Canada.

These early American unions focused on craftsmen like shoemakers and stone masons more than on laborers in factories. There was little effort to organize, or help the conditions of, the least-skilled workers.

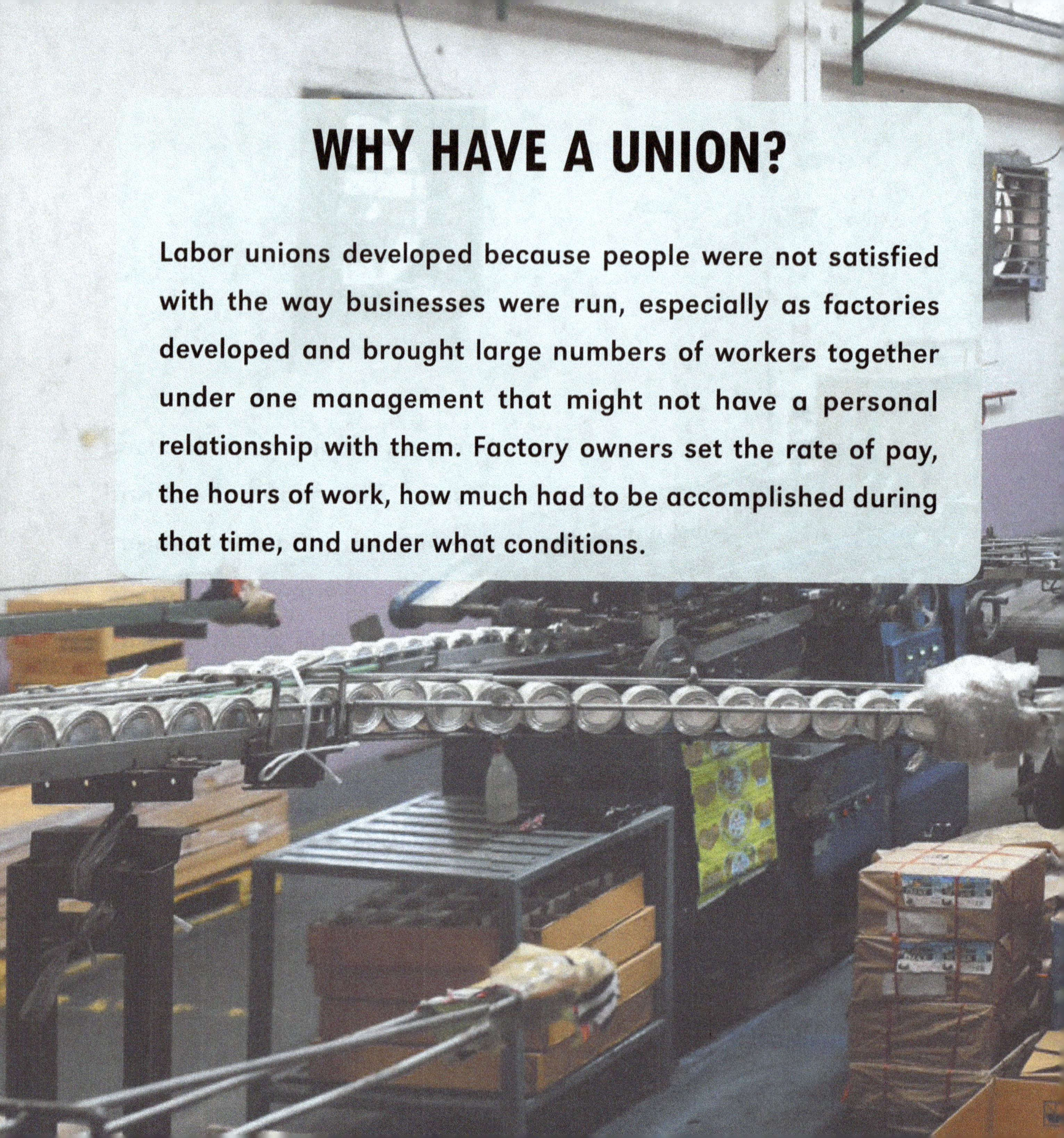

WHY HAVE A UNION?

Labor unions developed because people were not satisfied with the way businesses were run, especially as factories developed and brought large numbers of workers together under one management that might not have a personal relationship with them. Factory owners set the rate of pay, the hours of work, how much had to be accomplished during that time, and under what conditions.

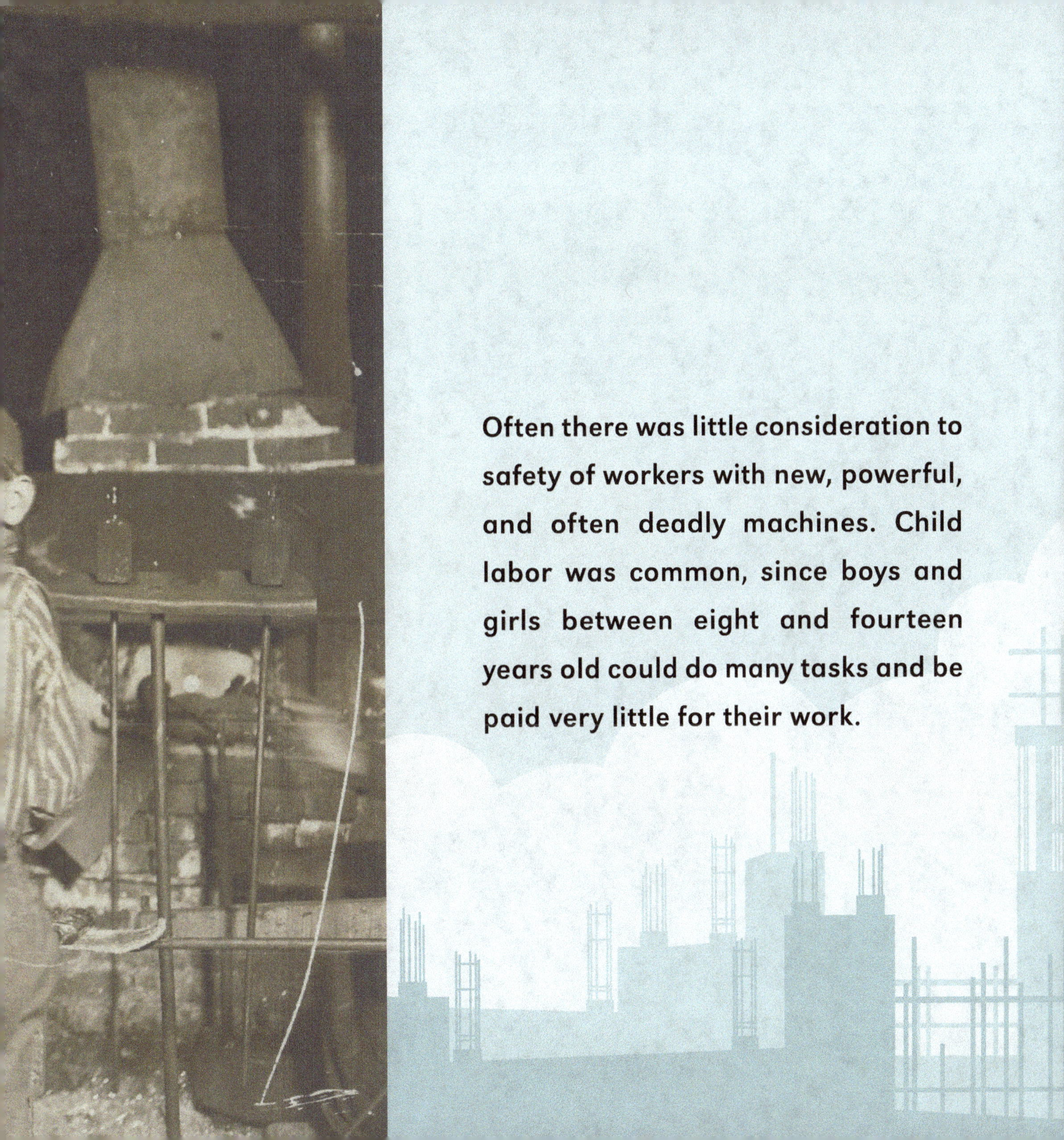

Often there was little consideration to safety of workers with new, powerful, and often deadly machines. Child labor was common, since boys and girls between eight and fourteen years old could do many tasks and be paid very little for their work.

TT 016 E
TT 021 E

If a single worker complained about the working conditions, the rate of pay, or some other issue, that worker would probably be fired. Having a union meant that each worker did not have to stand up for themselves alone.

BATTLE INFRONT OF ANTIOCH

When the union presented an issue, it also presented a consequence: if this thing is not resolved, we may stop working. You may not be able to produce your goods or make your money. Would it not be less expensive and less trouble to fix this thing than to try to resist making the change?

Often, owners resisted addressing the issue the union presented far longer than seems reasonable today. Owners would bring in strike-breakers, both non-union laborers to work the machines and thugs with weapons to attack the striking workers on their picket lines or even in their homes. For many employers, having any sort of limit on what they could do, and how much profit they could make, seemed a violation of their rights.

However, many other owners and employers came to see the sense of having a good working relationship with the union that their workers belonged to. Coming to an agreement that raised the hourly wage a little might cost the owners additional money, but it would also maintain production of the good or service that could be sold to make more money. A better-paid workforce also meant more people who could buy the factory's product!

FIGHTING FOR THE RIGHTS OF WORKERS

As North America became more and more industrialized, unions reached out more and more to factory workers, workers on trains, street sweepers, and other workers who did the everyday tasks of keeping the economy moving. Unions campaigned for ending child labor, providing health and retirement benefits to workers, making safer working conditions, and reducing the work week to forty hours.

au TREPORT
La Marée Tréportaise
rivages journaliers de poissons
Plateaux de Fruits de Mer
Tel : 02.35.86.81.19
Poissonnerie
de la côte d'Albâtre
02.35 82 83 68

FORMER AMERICAN FEDERATION OF LABOR BUILDING
James M. Wood
Union

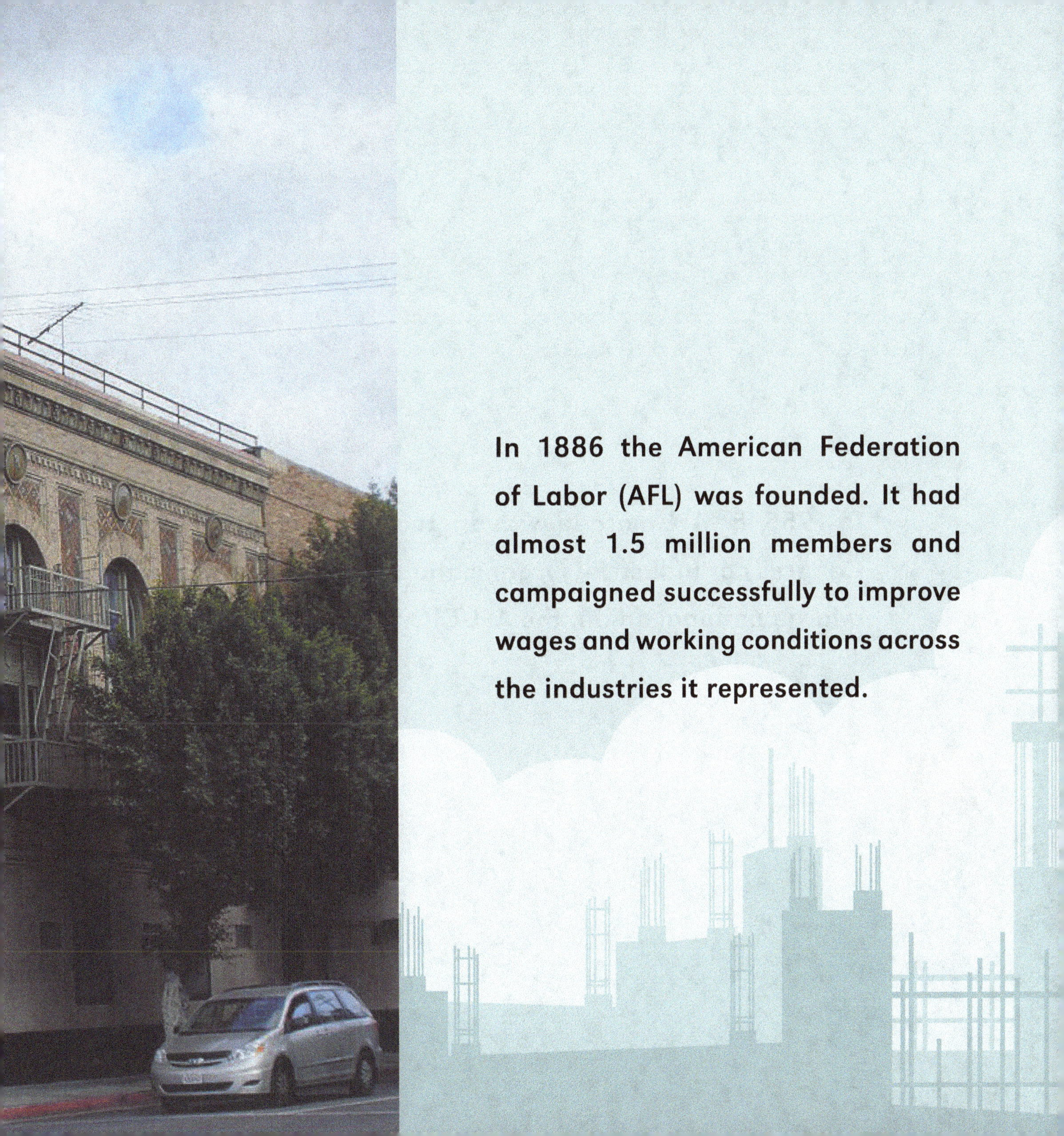

In 1886 the American Federation of Labor (AFL) was founded. It had almost 1.5 million members and campaigned successfully to improve wages and working conditions across the industries it represented.

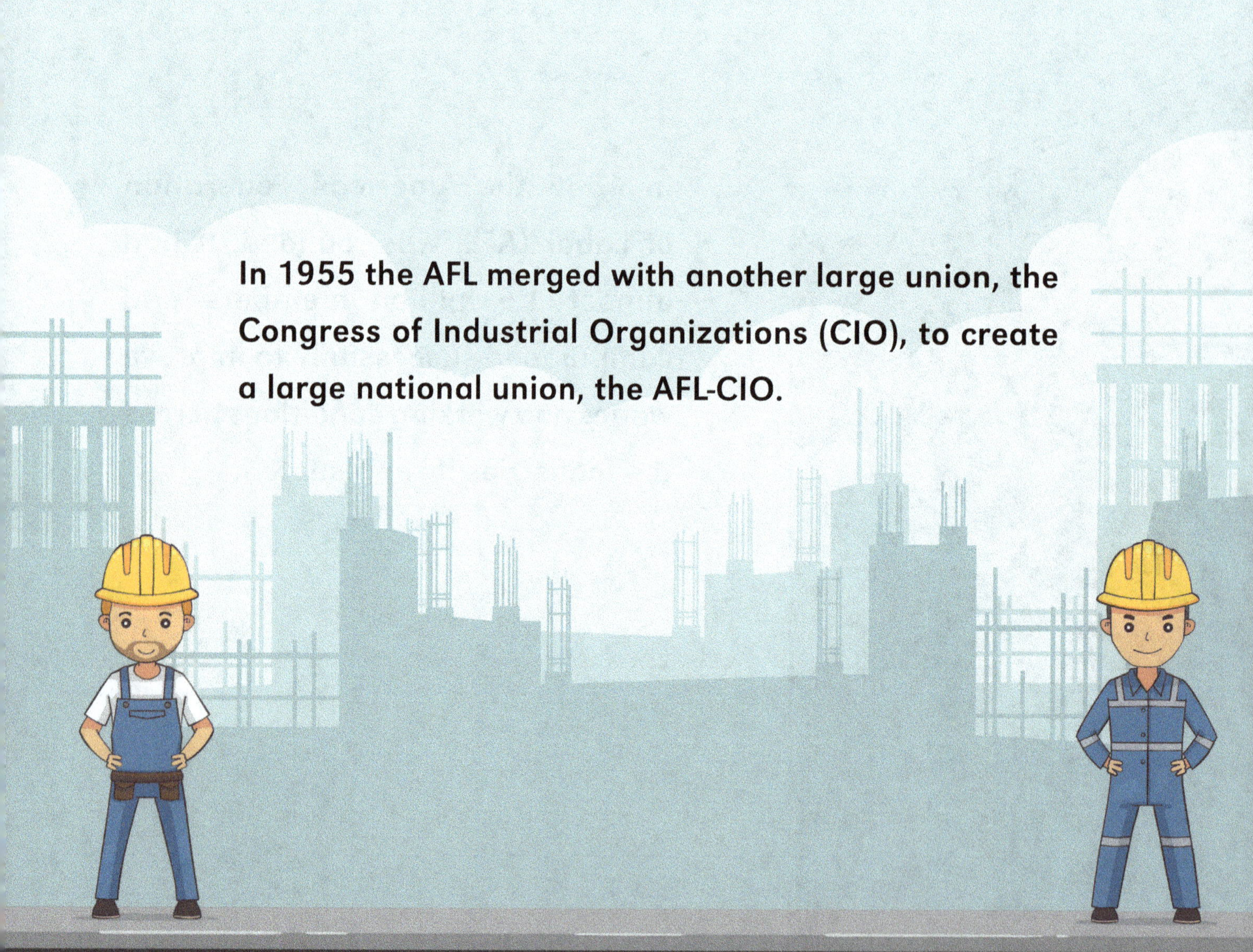

In 1955 the AFL merged with another large union, the Congress of Industrial Organizations (CIO), to create a large national union, the AFL-CIO.

ORIGINAL AFL HEADQUARTERS

UNIONS TODAY

Union membership in the United States and Canada reached its peak around 1970. In the United States at that time, about one third of workers were represented by unions.

The North American economy began a move toward knowledge-based work, like computer programming, and service work, and away from manufacturing. As factories closed and their work went to factories in other countries where the cost of labor was cheaper, millions of unionized jobs disappeared. There was also a concerted effort by business groups and the wealthy to depict unions as corrupt and somehow un-American. This, combined with laws in many states that make it harder to organize a union, have cut into the union movement. Now about 11 percent of the North American labor force is unionized.

THANK A UNION FOR THIS

It is worth remembering many things that unions worked for that we now take for granted. When unions were campaigning for these causes, many of them were considered too expensive or too idealistic.

Would you like to do without anything on this list?

↳ Weekends

↳ Lunch breaks and bathroom breaks during the work day

↳ Paid vacations

↳ Sick leave

↳ Social Security

↳ A minimum wage

↳ Equal pay for work of equal value

↳ An end to employer discrimination based on race, gender, religion, or national origin

Extra pay for overtime work
Restrictions on child labor
Health and safety regulations in the workplace
A forty-hour week

⇨ The right to bargain as a unit, rather than each worker having to bargain with the boss
⇨ Unemployment insurance
⇨ And many others!

CELEBRATE LABOR

Each year in the United States there are two days when people think a lot about workers and unions, and celebrate the contributions workers make to their countries. These days are May 1 (May Day) and the first Monday in September. Find out about these two holidays in the Baby Professor book Who Started the Labor Day Celebration?

Visit
BABY PROFESSOR
EDUCATION KIDS
www.BabyProfessorBooks.com
to download Free Baby Professor eBooks
and view our catalog of new and exciting
Children's Books

* 9 7 9 8 8 6 9 4 3 4 9 9 9 *